Native Americans

Cherokee Indians

Suzanne Morgan Williams

Heinemann Library
Chicago, Illinois

© 2003 Heinemann Library
a division of Reed Elsevier Inc.
Chicago, Illinois

Customer Service 888-454-2279

Visit our website at www.heinemannlibrary.com

Photo research by Alan Gottlieb
Printed and bound in the United States by Lake Book Manufacturing, Inc.

07 06 05 04 03
10 9 8 7 6 5 4 3 2 1

Library of Congress Cataloging-in-Publication Data
Williams, Suzanne, 1949-
   Cherokee Indians / Suzanne Morgan Williams.
      v. cm. -- (Native Americans)
Includes bibliographical references and index.
Contents: A Smokey sunrise -- Cherokee beginnings -- Forest life --
Cherokee towns -- Growing up Cherokee -- Medicine men and chiefs --
Fighting for themselves -- Living with the American frontier -- Writing
laws and language -- The Trail of Tears -- A new home, new problems --
Losing land, keeping old ways -- Today -- Cherokee, always.
   ISBN 1-40340-301-5 (lib. bdg.) -- ISBN 1-40340-508-5 (pbk.)
   1. Cherokee Indians--History--Juvenile literature. 2. Cherokee
Indians--Social life and customs--Juvenile literature. [1. Cherokee
Indians. 2. Indians of North America--Southern States.] I. Title. II.
Series. III. Native Americans (Heinemann Library (Firm))
   E99.C5 W59 2002
   975.004'9755--dc21

                          2002006127

Acknowledgments
The author and publisher are grateful to the following for permission to reproduce copyright material: pp. 4, 5, 28, 29 Marilyn "Angel"
Wynn/Nativestock; p. 6 Frank H. McClung Museum, University of Tennessee; p. 7 Dorothy Sullivan, Memory Circle Studio, Norman,
Oklahoma; p. 8 Museum of the Cherokee Indian; p. 8 inset National Anthropological Archives, Smithsonian Institution; pp. 9, 22, 23
Murv Jacob, Tahlequah, Oklahoma; p. 10 Frank H. McClung Museum, University of Tennessee/drawing by James R. Whyte; p. 11 Frank
H. McClung Museum, University of Tennessee/painting by Carlyle Viello; pp. 12, 14, 27 National Museum of the American Indian,
Smithsonian Institution; p. 13 National Museum of American Art/Art Resource; p. 15 The Thomas Gilcrease Institute of American
History and Art, Tulsa, Oklahoma; pp. 16, 20 Library of Congress; pp. 17, 19 National Anthropological Archives, Smithsonian Institution;
p. 18 Chief Vann House Historic Site; p. 21 National Portrait Gallery, Smithsonian Institution/Art Resource; p. 24 Philbrook Museum of
Art, Tulsa Oklahoma; p. 25T Museum of the Cherokee Indian; p. 25B Western History Collections, University of Oklahoma Libraries;
p. 26 Archives and Manuscripts Division, Oklahoma Historical Society; p. 30 Michal Heron.

Cover image by Murv Jacob, Tahlequah, Oklahoma.

"Why We Dance," (p. 9) by MariJo Moore originally published in *Whispering Wind Magazine*, Vol. 31, No. 5, 2001. More information
available at www.marijomoore.com.

Special thanks to Lisa LaRue Stopp, Wadulisi Dinalewisda, for her help in the preparation of this book.

Some words are shown in bold, **like this.** You can find out
what they mean by looking in the glossary.

Contents

A Smoky Sunrise

Mist hangs in the forest. A creek bubbles down the hillside. A deer sniffs the air. It steps quietly into the trees. The sun warms the hillside in the Smoky Mountains, in the southeast of the United States. This is the Cherokee people's **homeland.** They call themselves *Ani Tsalagi* (say it like this: ah-NEE Jal-ah-GEE).

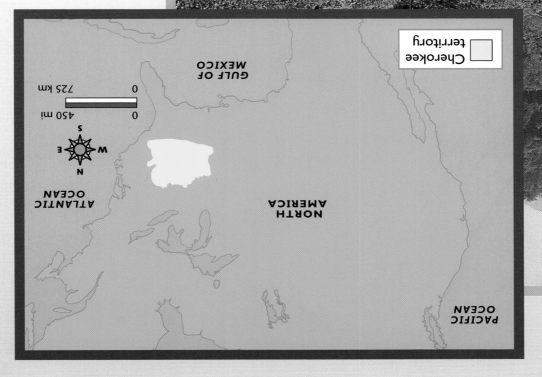

Cherokee territory

ATLANTIC
OCEAN

NORTH
AMERICA

GULF OF
MEXICO

PACIFIC
OCEAN

0   450 mi
0   725 Km

Their **ancestors** lived here for hundreds, and maybe thousands, of years. They hunted in the forests. They planted corn, beans, and other crops. They planted in the valleys and by the streams. The Cherokees' ancestors were Woodland Indians. They were **ancient** people who lived as part of this forested land.

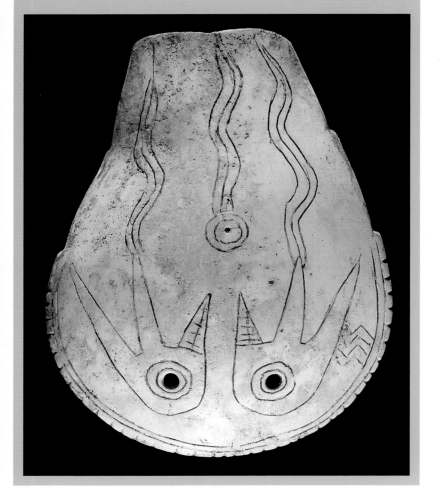

This shell was carved hundreds of years ago by a Cherokee craftsperson.

A Long History

Scientists think Cherokees have lived in today's Georgia, Alabama, Tennessee, and Carolinas for at least 3,000 years. **Ancient** people may have lived in the area more than 9,000 years ago.

Cherokee Beginnings

Some Cherokees say that their **ancestors** came to the area around the Smoky Mountains long ago. They came from the north. No matter where the Cherokees came from, the Smoky Mountains and the plains below them were home.

One story says **The Great One** created the first man
in the Smoky Mountains. The Great One saw that he
needed company and planted a seed nearby. The seed
grew into a beautiful corn plant with an ear of corn
at the top. The first woman stepped from that corn.
She is called Selu, Corn Woman.

*This is Selu, Corn Woman. Cherokees honor
corn and women. Both give life.*

Forest Life

The Cherokees knew the plants and animals of their **homeland.** Men hunted animals such as deer, bears, and **elk.** Women planted fields of corn, beans, and squash. They called these plants *tsoi unadalvi,* or "the three sisters." Cherokees knew when to plant and hunt as the seasons changed.

This Cherokee man is hunting with a blow gun and darts. Cherokees believe people and animals are related. They ask animals to forgive them for hunting.

Each season has its celebrations and dances. There are seven **sacred** dances. The Green Corn **Ceremony** happens in summer. It celebrates the first ripe corn. The New Moon Ceremony in October welcomes a new year. The Cherokees gathered in towns for celebrations.

*Today, about 600 Cherokees follow the **traditional religion**. Many more dance and celebrate together.*

9

Cherokee Towns

Four hundred years ago, there were about 200 Cherokee towns. Most towns had 30 to 60 houses. Cherokee families built neat, round homes. They pounded long, thin branches into the ground. They tied them together at the top and wove more branches around this frame. Then they filled in the spaces with mud and **plaster**.

In the winter, Cherokees lived in covered houses like the one on the left. When it got warmer, they moved into open houses like the one on the right.

This picture of a Cherokee farm was painted in the 1700s.
It shows both summer and winter houses.

When a Cherokee man married, he moved to his wife's home. Sometimes they built a new house near her family. Cherokee women owned the crops and the houses. When a woman died, her daughters kept her home. A woman's brothers would help raise her children.

Little People

Cherokees say that "little people" with white hair hide in rocks and by waterfalls. They like to play tricks, and they also watch over children. Their Cherokee name is *yvnwi usdi* (yuhn-WEE oos-DEE).

Growing Up Cherokee

Every child is born into a **clan,** or family group. Babies belong to their mother's clan. Cherokee clans help each other. Men and women of the same clan are not allowed to marry each other. At one time, there were more than ten clans. Some of these clans joined together, and now there are seven clans.

Cherokee Clans

Wolf	*Ani Waya*
Deer	*Ani Awi*
Paint	*Ani Wodi*
Bird	*Ani Tsiskwa*
Long Hair	*Ani Gilohi*
Blue	*Ani Sahoni*
Wild Potato	*Ani Gotagewi*

The Cherokee child in this 1907 photograph is part of her mother's clan.

*Cherokee chief Black Coat, shown here in an 1834 painting, is wearing both European and **traditional** Cherokee clothes.*

Boys learned to hunt from their fathers and uncles. Girls learned to plant, cook, and make clothing from their mothers, grandmothers, and aunts. Cherokee children learned to share what they had. They shared with their family, clan, and village. When people helped each other, everyone lived better.

Medicine Men and Chiefs

Medicine men know the ceremonies that help keep people happy and healthy. They heal sick people with **herbs.** But in 1540, Europeans arrived. Indians caught European **diseases** from them. Indians' bodies could not fight the new diseases, and medicine men could not cure them. These diseases killed about 150,000 Cherokees. In 1674, there were about 50,000 Cherokee left.

A gourd rattle like the one below is used when Cherokee medicine men and ceremonial chiefs sing.

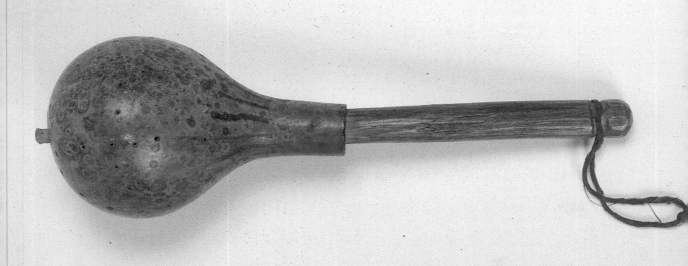

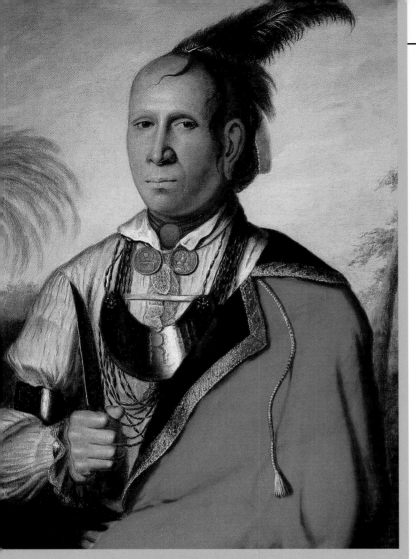

In 1762, Cherokee leader Cunne Shote met with English leaders in London, England.

Each Cherokee town had a white chief for peaceful times. It also had a red chief for wars. These leaders were respected, powerful men. They helped solve problems in their communities and talked with other tribes. Sometimes tribes fought over hunting grounds, a robbery, or murder.

Fighting for Themselves

In the 1600s, Europeans began living on the coast. They did not share the land as the Cherokees did. The Europeans cleared big fields. They pushed other tribes into the Cherokee **homeland.**

Chief Oostenaco commanded the Cherokees during the French and Indian Wars (1689–1763).

These Cherokee leaders traveled to England in 1730. They are dressed in English clothing that was given to them.

In the 1600s and 1700s, Cherokees fought many battles to keep their lands. They fought other tribes, French traders, and **settlers.** They fought for and against the United States. In each war, the chiefs decided whose side to take. They fought to **protect** the Cherokee people and their lands.

In Their Own Words:

"We will never let this land go. To let it go will be like throwing away (our) mother that gave birth (to us)."
—Aitooweyah writing to Cherokee chief John Ross

17

Living with the American Frontier

Settlers from the coast kept moving west. Cherokees sold them some land. Other land was taken in wars. Still, the Cherokees kept a lot of their **homeland.** As the settlers moved closer, life changed for the Cherokees. They began to dress more like the settlers, and many Cherokee families built log cabins.

Some Cherokee families earned a lot of money with their farms. They built mansions like this one, which belonged to Chief James Vann.

Some Cherokee people built log cabins and lived like settlers.

Some Cherokee people learned to speak English. Some married white people. **Missionaries** came, and some Cherokees became **Christian.** Many learned to farm and **weave.** Some families built farms and bought **slaves.** They lived like southern **plantation** owners. Some Cherokees decided to sell their land to the United States. They moved away from the settlers to present-day Arkansas.

In Their Own Words:
"When we entered into treaties with the whites, our brothers, their whole cry is, 'More land!'"
—Onitositaii, Cherokee chief

Writing Laws and Language

The Cherokee **homeland** was already a nation. In 1827, Cherokees wrote a **constitution,** a plan for their government. They created courts like the ones in the United States. They elected a **council** to make laws. They built a capital, New Echota, in present-day Georgia.

This is the title page of the Cherokee constitution, written in the Cherokee language.

This painting of Sequoyah with his syllabary was made by Henry Inman around 1830.

Sequoyah, whose English name was George Guess, wanted Cherokee people to be able to read and write their own language. Sequoyah matched a letter or other **symbol** to each sound in Cherokee. He created a written language, or **syllabary,** by himself. He finished the syllabary in 1821. Many Cherokees only needed three or four days to learn to read Sequoyah's syllabary.

The Phoenix

By 1828, Cherokees had their own newspaper called *The Phoenix*. It was printed in English and Cherokee.

The Trail of Tears

Cherokees lived a lot like their white neighbors. However, Cherokee land had rich soil, **timber,** and gold. Miners poured into the Cherokee Nation. The state of Georgia decided that it wanted Cherokee lands. Georgia **officials** gave Cherokee farms to Georgians. They put Cherokee leaders and **missionaries** in jail.

This image shows the Trail of Tears as it was painted by modern Cherokee artist Murv Jacob.

In 1838, the United States government ordered Cherokees to leave their homes and move west. Most Cherokees refused to go. Their leader was Principal Chief John Ross. However, the U.S. Army rounded them up. Sixteen thousand Cherokees were forced to walk 800 miles (1,287 kilometers) to Indian Territory in present-day Oklahoma. As many as 4,000 Cherokees died because of the trip, which was later called the Trail of Tears.

23

New Home, New Problems

It was difficult to **settle** in Indian Territory. Many Cherokees had lost almost everything they owned. They were angry at the group of people in their tribe who signed the **Treaty** of New Echota. That treaty sold their **homeland** to the United States. Different groups of Cherokees fought for control of the tribe.

Principal Chief John Ross signed the Treaty of 1846, which stopped fighting among different groups of Cherokees.

These Cherokee men fought for the southern states in the Civil War.

Some Cherokees gave this beaded belt to the United States government to show they agreed to sell their land.

The fighting stopped with the Treaty of 1846. Cherokees tried to build new farms and new lives. In 1861, the **Civil War** started. Many Cherokees fought for the South, but the North won. The United States government punished Cherokees by giving much of their land to other tribes.

Losing Land, Keeping Old Ways

By 1905, the United States government was dividing Indian lands. Each Indian family got land for a farm. The rest of the Indian lands were sold to white **settlers.** In 1907, most of Indian Territory became the state of Oklahoma.

On September 16, 1893, white settlers raced into the former Cherokee territory in Oklahoma to claim land.

*This photograph shows the Cherokee Tribal **Council** in 1899.*

Some Cherokees refused to take the divided land. They wanted to share land as they always had. Redbird Smith was their leader. He helped them remember their **customs, religion,** and **clan** system. Cherokees had carried a flame called the **Sacred** Fire from their **homeland.** They never let this flame go out. By 1905, the Sacred Fire was burning at 22 places in the Cherokee Nation. The Sacred Fire still burns today.

Today

Today, many Cherokees live in the Cherokee Nation in Oklahoma. Others live on **traditional** lands in North Carolina, Georgia, Tennessee, or Alabama. Cherokee people live and dress like everyone else. Many Cherokees work in health care. Others package food. Cherokees are farmers, scientists, and jet pilots.

This Cherokee firefighter is giving a special demonstration.

28

Stickball is still played today by both girls and boys.

Cherokees remember their traditions. Some keep alive their **ancient ceremonies** and dances. They also meet at events such as **powwows** and the Cherokee National Holiday. At these times, women may wear **tear dresses**. Cherokee artists **weave** baskets the way their grandmothers did. Other artists make traditional ball sticks for stickball games.

Stickball

Early Cherokees played stickball, or *anetsodi* (aw-nay-JOE-dee). Some Cherokees still play stickball. They play on a field with a tall pole in the middle. Teams get points for hitting the pole with a tiny ball, or for hitting a wooden fish on top of the pole.

Always Cherokee

The Cherokee Nation has 220,000 members. It is the second largest tribe in the United States. Cherokees are working to keep their language alive. The tribe helps people get health care and jobs. A factory in the Cherokee Nation in Oklahoma is going to start building motorcycles. What are they called? Cherokee Motorcycles! Today, Cherokee people work to keep their **traditions**. They respect the land. They will always be Cherokee.

*This teacher is teaching the Cherokee language using the **syllabary** that Sequoyah made in 1821.*

Glossary

ancestor   relative who lived long before someone's parents and grandparents

ancient   very old

carve   cut into a shape with a knife or sharp tool

ceremony   event that celebrates a special occasion

Christian   person who follows a religion based on the teachings of Jesus

Civil War   war between northern and southern states from 1861 to1865

clan   group of families that are related

constitution   plan for government

council   group of leaders who make decisions for a group of people

custom   something that has been done for a long time

disease   sickness

elk   large animal that looks like a deer but is much bigger

herb   plant that can be used as medicine

homeland   place where a group of people come from

medicine man   person with spiritual power

missionary   person who teaches others about religion

official   person with power to carry out rules

plantation   large farm. People who worked there were often slaves.

plaster   mud that dries smooth and white

powwow   Indian gathering or celebration

protect   keep from harm or danger

religion   system of spiritual beliefs and practices

sacred   holy; something that has special meaning for a community or tribe

settle   make a home in a new place. A person who does this is a settler.

slave   person who was bought and sold as a worker

syllabary   list of written symbols that expresses a language

symbol   something that stands for something else

tear dress   traditional Cherokee dress worn after the Trail of Tears

The Great One   creator of everything

timber   trees that can be cut for wood

traditional   using the old ways

treaty   agreement between governments or groups of people

weave   lace together threads or other material

31

More Books to Read

Bruchac, Joseph. *The Trail of Tears.* New York: Random House Books for Young Readers, 1999.

Burgan, Michael. *Trail of Tears.* Minneapolis: Compass Point Books, 2001.

Press, Petra. *The Cherokee.* Minneapolis: Compass Point Books, 2001.

Santella, Andrew. *The Cherokee: American Indians.* Danbury, Conn.: Scholastic Library Publishing, 2001.

Todd, Anne M. *The Cherokee: An Independent Nation.* Minnetonka, Minn.: Capstone Press, Incorporated, 2002.

Index